A PHOTOGRAPHIC SAFARI

AFRICAN WILDLIFE

A PHOTOGRAPHIC SAFARI

AFRICAN WILDLIFE

STEPHEN J. KRASEMANN

BARBARA BACH

NorthWord Press
Minnetonka, Minnesota

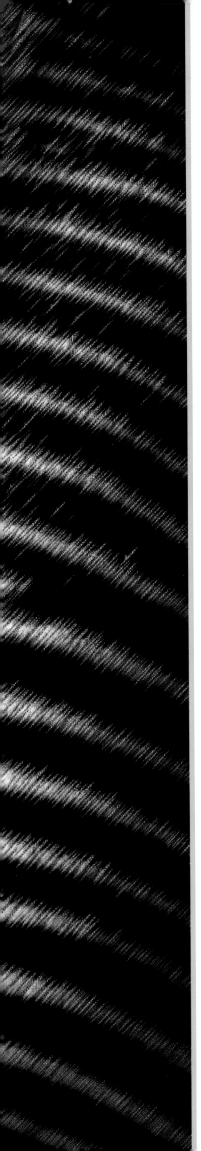

DEDICATION

*I would like to dedicate this book with best wishes
for all our wildlife and our planet in the coming years.*

Text © Stephen J. Krasemann and Barbara Bach, 1998
Photography © Stephen J. Krasemann, 1998

NorthWord Press
5900 Green Oak Drive
Minnetonka, MN 55343
1-800-328-3895

Book design by Russell S. Kuepper

Front cover photos: Zebra back coat; Masai giraffe (left inset); elephant (center inset); cheetah
(right inset). Page 2 photo: Female vervet monkey nursing her young. Back cover photo:
Acacia tree.

Library of Congress Cataloging-in-Publication Data
Krasemann, Stephen J.
   African Wildlife : a photographic safari/Stephen J. Krasemann,
Barbara Bach.
     p. cm.
  ISBN 1-55971-668-1
  1. Wildlife photography--Africa. 2. Zoology--Africa--Pictorial
works. I. Bach, Barbara. II. Title.
TR729.W54K73 1998
591.96--dc21   98-23821

Printed in Singapore
02 01 00 99 98 / 5 4 3 2 1

INTRODUCTION

I remember how silent an elephant walks. And how the sun seems to dive below the horizon at sunset only to rocket into the sky at dawn. I recall the hippopotamuses "laughing" in the muddy river at midday. And the spot of red in the distance that materialized into a Masai walking over the savannah.

Africa bombards the senses—smells, sights, sounds. Each sense combines to create a special feeling, a mosaic of Africa. Each person has his or her own impressions from Africa; perhaps it is the incessant cooing of doves, the maniacal laugh of the hyenas, or lions roaring in the darkness.

Once you have visited Africa, pieces of your experience will always be there, at the edge of your thoughts, ready to be shared with others who have traveled there or who desire to visit Africa for the first time.

Africa is one of those "dream destinations."

I longed to travel there since first seeing the movie Born Free.

I was in love with the bigger-than-life animals.

Africa breathed adventure with a hint of danger.

Now that I've been to various African countries, my dream is reality. And this is what draws people to visit and revisit Africa's savannahs and jungles—Africa really is an adventure with a hint of danger.

Most visitors have already read the book or watched the movie based on the life of Karen Blixen, *Out of Africa.* Then they experience Africa's wildlife through the window of a Land Rover or mini-bus. They peer into the eyes of lions, elephants and hyenas. And they are forever affected by their travels, the game, the food, the sun and the wind.

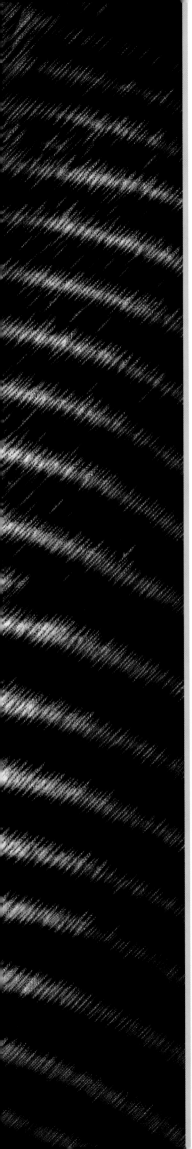

There are so many positive reasons for visiting Africa that any negatives are but mere inconveniences that one endures when traveling to any international destination. To minimize those negatives, I prepare well for a photographic safari to Africa.

I begin by making a list of all the items I need to assemble and errands I must do. Then there are those dreaded inoculations, but they aren't really that bad. And a visa application often takes several weeks to process.

Plenty of cash, credit cards or traveler's checks is a must. I also pack a small first-aid kit that includes prescription drugs for intestinal upset, antibiotics and pain killers—just in case.

I bring an ample supply of sweets. They are most appreciated by drivers and other people you meet. If I'm hoping to carry any gifts on my return, I make room in my baggage by bringing clothes I plan to give away as gifts on my travels. Those clothes never go to waste; in fact, they often make excellent bartering items.

Remember to try to travel as light as possible, but to bring everything you will need for your safari. This seemingly contradictory advice means you should bring all your film and batteries for the entire trip. You can't count on readily buying exotic photographic supplies in Africa. I usually expect to expose five rolls of film daily, although sometimes I have exposed over twenty rolls in a single day.

This may sound like a lot of film; but just think, if you have a chance to photograph animals like elephants, lions, giraffes and hippos, you won't want to run out of film. And that's just the beginning. You will probably also see hyenas, cheetahs, leopards, zebras, wildebeest, buffalo, warthogs, baboons, rhinos, ostriches, gazelles, antelope. And of course you will want to photograph lots of scenics, sunrises and sunsets, plus your traveling companions. So if you expose just three rolls per subject on this small list, you would need sixty rolls.

You will expose more film than you ever thought possible.

On my way home, I hand-carry my exposed film. I can replace every other item of baggage, but I refuse to jeopardize those precious moments on film. My brand of film has varied over the years, but the bulk of it has been slide film in the ASA 64-100 range. I also carry a few rolls of higher speed film for those times around sunrise and sunset when I want to capture subjects in dim light.

I take at least two camera bodies because if your camera quits, that's the end of your photographic experience. I do ninety-eight percent of my photography in Africa with an 80-200mm zoom and a 200-400 zoom lens. I also carry a couple other zoom lenses—a 20-35mm and a 35-70mm— and a 1.4X telextender.

Since travel conditions can be dusty, I take plenty of lens cleaning supplies. I always cover my cameras with a shirt or camera case when traveling in the vehicle. I also recommend a camera window mount that can be folded flat to use out the vehicle roof hatch.

Here's one final photo tip. Don't harass wildlife by approaching too close. Animals walking away with their rear ends facing the camera aren't nearly as appealing as an animal coming toward you. So try to stop well ahead of your subject and let it come to you for a more natural photograph.

If Africa is one of your "dream destinations,"
we hope this book becomes the beginning of your journey.

Barbara Bach

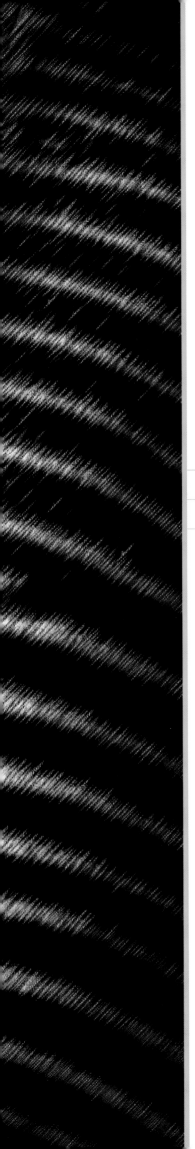

THERE IS A RICKETY OLD OUTHOUSE BY OUR CAMP. Butterflies fly out of the seat hole when you enter; there's also a swallow's nest on the ceiling and a view over the Serengeti Veldt.

But I have to write about a terrifying moment this morning. We were photographing a pride of seven simba (lions). As we approached, all lion heads were lifted, eyes alert, looking toward us. Only seconds after we stopped, all simba were flat down with eyes closed; they knew we were tourists.

So, as I was lamenting the fact I couldn't receive any lion's attention, I adjusted my tripod leg with a loud metallic click. In an instant, the nearest female lion was coiled and prepared to spring at me just twenty yards distant. She was growling and staring directly at me perched atop our Land Rover.

I was scared. I didn't know what to do. I froze.

Two leaps and she would have me.

She refused to calm down. We didn't know what to do. The whole pride was alert, waiting for this lioness to respond. Eventually, our driver chose to start the engine for an immediate getaway. All worked well and we escaped, but we had to drive quite a distance before the lioness relaxed.

I realized my tripod clicking had been interpreted as a clacking of jaws—an aggressive sound. An intense situation, let me tell you.

JOURNAL ENTRY

We're deep within the Serengeti looking for cheetah, without luck. We have stopped to picnic upon a large rock; animals are visible in all directions.

Rained much of today; a poor day, photographic-wise. Lots of marginal light shots.

Intense stare and total concentration are traits of this lioness focused on her potential meal. Each movement by predator or prey can mean life or death.

JOURNAL ENTRY

A very long day of photography—12 hours of photographing an eagle owl, warthog, lion, a wolf spider, rock hyrax, rainbow lizard, white-crowned shrike, hippo faces, cape buffalo, kori bustard, bat-eared fox, giraffe, lilac-breasted roller, Thompson's gazelle and Eland.

Drove three hours from Seronera to Kerewera, only to find the whole area recently burned.

Dusssty . . . everywhere, all the time, and this equatorial sun is intense, even if this is the cool season.

Very, very few mosquitoes and flies. Breezes blow almost continuously. It's 6:20 p.m., and the sun is nearing the horizon; it's still white, white light. At sunrise, the sun literally seems to spring into the sky.

JOURNAL ENTRY

Africa looks as we imagined it in our mind's eye during the dry season—brown broken grasses and gray dust paling the landscape.

My hair is dusty, knotted by the wind and like straw from the sun. My skin is the same.

As we came upon this scene, I quickly maneuvered the Land Rover, framing the vulture in the background clouds before the bird could fly away.

Climbing acacia trees can be hazardous. Notice the thorn in this hyrax's rear leg.

Overleaf: Large, old, solitary cape buffalo bulls often spend their lives tucked away in dense vegetation.

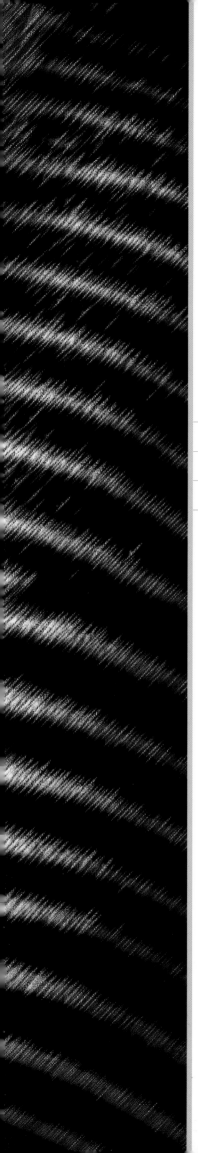

These plains are rough on the body, sun so bright, wind ever blowing and dust puffing up at every step. But if you have to ask me why I do this, and why I love this life, I can honestly not give you a satisfactory answer.

But then, if you have to ask such a question, you'll never understand my answer.

JOURNAL ENTRY

The day began when our most elusive animal to date became our most cooperative animal to photograph.

A male duma (cheetah) chased and killed an African hare, ate the hare, cleaned, yawned and walked off into the grasses right in front of the camera.

Hot midday on the plain and in our camp. Buffalo and topi graze the distant hill and I wait for the more interesting afternoon light.

It's too hot for me to nap so I stretch in the shade of an acacia tree. This is our last day here; tomorrow and the next day are moves to Ndutu and Ngorongoro. The Land Rover is rough on bodies; no heat on cool mornings, plus very rugged springs.

The one thing I miss here is physical exercise and walking. Our driver is great for letting me out to stalk. But there's little walking allowed for fear of hidden predators. Interesting situation, but my body doesn't feel as healthy without the rigor of hiking, climbing and exertion.

There's a baboon walking warily around me as I write.

When they're not hunting, large cats can usually be found napping. This cheetah has just awakened.

Overleaf: Heading out for the hunt, a cheetah uses the grass for cover whenever possible. Cheetahs hunt mainly during daylight hours.

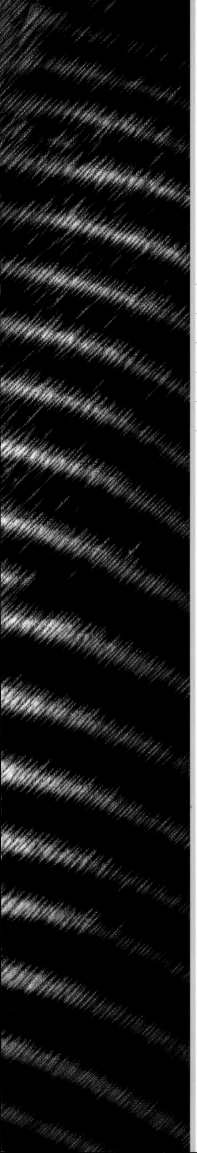

JOURNAL ENTRY

A small band of zebras came to the edge of the soda lake to sip a bit of its mineral waters; flamingos made for a beautiful out-of-focus background.

After exposing a roll of film, we noticed two lionesses heading in our direction. The zebras hadn't noticed the lionesses.

As the lionesses stalked directly at our Land Rover, we noticed movement in the distant grasses. From their location along the lake, other lionesses were sneaking in toward the lake's edge, forming a semicircle in an attempt to close off one exit route along the lakeshore.

"The zebras hadn't noticed the lionesses."

*"For a few moments all the action
was lost in a cloud of dust."*

By now, the two lead lionesses were lying flat in the grasses, one on either side of our vehicle; we didn't dare do anything. One lioness began to move toward the other side of the lake's edge. She was closing the net on the zebras.

At her chosen moment, first the lead lioness, then the other lioness both took off at a full run toward the zebras.

For a few moments all the action was lost in a cloud of dust. The zebras were cut off from escape from the far end of the lakeshore; now they were headed back our way with all lions up and in pursuit. One zebra was knocked off balance when a lion grabbed onto its neck, but the zebra viciously bit the lion on the ear and was able to escape.

Another zebra was not so lucky. This one had a lion hugging its neck as it stood upright, in shock. Another lioness sat at the zebra's hindquarter, already having it hamstrung. This zebra wasn't going anywhere, but it wasn't going down, either.

A lioness hopped atop its back, while two other lionesses dangled from its neck, pulling in tandem, trying to topple the zebra.

It eventually took the concerted effort of five lionesses to knock the zebra off its feet. Then they could grip the zebra's windpipe, causing it to pass out and die.

What an amazing, fortunate, fantastic circumstance of luck. Two zebras were ultimately killed to feed seventeen lions. I photographed the chase and the aftermath. Thirty-one rolls, that's over 1,000 pictures; I can count on one hand the times I have shot this much film in one sitting.

The beginning of the end . . . The zebra crumples under the lion's assault . . .
The last moments of the zebra's life are spent in shock. Death comes quickly.

Overleaf: The zebra dies so the lions can live.

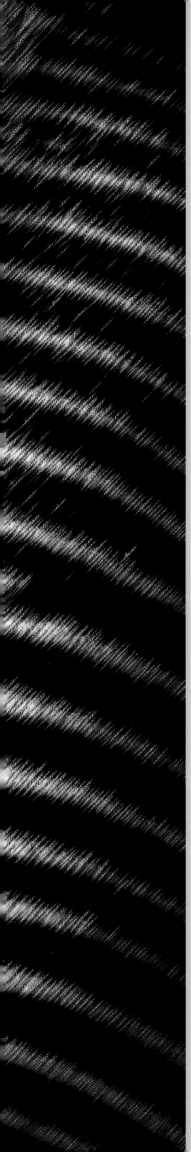

JOURNAL ENTRY

Today we gathered firewood with a borrowed saw, and then two female simba came right into camp to drink.

At the start of our afternoon game drive, we ran into four bull eland. These elusive largest antelope were smack full frame in my camera. On we went into a nice buffalo herd with cattle egrets and red-billed oxpeckers (camp was still in sight). While we were photographing the buffalo, we noticed a Grant's gazelle with a two- or three-day-old spindly-legged young. I walked up and could have touched it in the grass.

There are at least three separate giraffes staring me down.

Giraffes look like slow-motion film when they run.

JOURNAL ENTRY - NGORONGORO CRATER

We drove to the back of this sunken volcanic crater and were beginning to photograph wildebeest when a stampede broke out. We knew we hadn't caused it. Driving on, we found the cause—three male lions had killed two wildebeest. This kill was not as photogenic as our earlier zebra kill, but photos were obviously taken.

Tonight, our last in the crater, is calm. The air carries shrieking sounds of baboons settling off to sleep, and the sound of crickets.

JOURNAL ENTRY

I've gained a small feeling for the situation of people and wildlife here in Tanzania. I sense the wildlife situation will last but a short while—seven years, maybe ten years—before rules prevent driving off the roads in Ngorongoro Crater. This safari's finish is in sight; I'd like to say, "Please, just a couple more days, another few hours, please."

With fluid movements, a running giraffe seems to float across the plains. This Masai giraffe came bounding out of the brush when it realized the other giraffes were moving off.

JOURNAL ENTRY - TARANGIRE

I've seen the Southern Cross constellation, felt the equatorial heat, the cool night breezes, and I've fallen in love with another part of the world.

The last of its kind in our world.

I won't forget these times, this adventure.

JOURNAL ENTRY

I think of the chores and the routine of being back home, and that thought seems so mundane compared to where I am now.

We are settling into our own routine here—rising by 6 a.m., a quick breakfast, a photo run, return to camp for lunch and an afternoon rest, then another photo run around 3 or 4, return by 7, dinner at 8, into bed by 9 or 10. Exhausted, happy.

The bush is the place to be.

Oxpeckers feed in the cracks and crevices of the rhino's hide removing ticks and other parasitic creatures.

When we used our binoculars to follow the two Grant's gazelles' gaze, we spotted two male lions almost a mile away.

Overleaf: These may look like identical Grevy's zebra twins, but each zebra's stripe pattern is unique unto itself.

JOURNAL ENTRY - NGORONGORO CRATER

A slow beginning. It takes me a few days to get my photographic edges functioning; in another day or two, I won't miss many photographs.

It's enjoyable to be sleeping in a tent so I can hear the wind and the animals, and smell the wood fire.

JOURNAL ENTRY

We find wildlife everywhere. So green, lots of dew. The sun is always intense; I'm being careful to watch for sunburn. So far, so good. I have some color, but it takes four days' sun stimulation for the body to produce melanin in protective amounts.

Rain clouds build and erupt in dense heavy thunderstorms each afternoon. It's pouring on my tent, cozy.

And as I lie here—quite content—the birds serenade me, perhaps into a dream.

Emerging from the waters below with a freshly caught fish, this pied kingfisher returns to feed on its favorite perch.

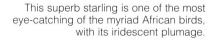

This superb starling is one of the most eye-catching of the myriad African birds, with its iridescent plumage.

JOURNAL ENTRY - NGORONGORO CRATER

An afternoon thunderstorm is booming across the eastern wall of the crater and obscures the landscape in a veil of gray rain. Winds cool the air, animals graze in the distance. And me? My mind ponders my place in all this. I visit, yet I feel I belong here; I could live here.

I collect photos to take with me. Ah, the memories, life's memories. That's what we have when years pass.

Memories are all we can really say are ours.

And the dreams and memories are enough.

The rain showers move closer; I'll retreat to my tent and ponder all these deep thoughts.

Dik-Diks are the smallest members of the antelope family, and are found in some of the driest regions in Africa.

The gerenuk has adapted to feed halfway between the grasses and the treetops.

Overleaf: Short rainstorms will water the vegetation, bringing nourishment to the parched Serengeti landscape.

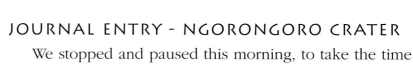

JOURNAL ENTRY - NGORONGORO CRATER

We stopped and paused this morning, to take the time one seldom takes to appreciate the morning solitude with the myriad grass-eating mammals, the resting predators and all the lively birds.

My last safari was a whirlwind. On this one I will make time to take in moments at a pace somewhat less than a blitz.

There is so much to absorb on one short safari to Africa. It's a pleasurable sensory overload. But one must take care to slow the pace, to take the time to appreciate the events and the creatures that make up the experience.

JOURNAL ENTRY

The Speke's weavers about our campsite have such an array of songs, overlaid with a background harmony—a real sound delight.

Feeling much better, although I'm not totally recovered from a bout of dehydration and diarrhea yet. I think coming from a winter environment and forcing my body to adapt to summer conditions has something to do with my ills.

I could really savor an ice-cold Pepsi.

Speke's weavers apparently can vocalize or sing two songs at the same time. This species' intricate grass nests usually dangle from branch ends over water.

Possessing one of the strongest jaws in nature, the spotted hyena has the power to crush bones to feed on the marrow inside.

*"Immediately, all the bulls encircled
the wounded lioness . . ."*

JOURNAL ENTRY
NGORONGORO CRATER

Off we went toward what we thought were cheetahs. Instead, they turned out to be hyenas with a freshly killed young wildebeest. Jackals were nearby and lions were moving our way. One lioness began trotting upon sighting the hyenas. She chased the hyena until it let go of the carcass, only to have a male lion chase her, attempting to steal her usurped hyena kill.

All this chasing attracted a herd of bachelor cape buffalos, which also took after the running lion and lioness.

As the buffalo bore down on the two lions, one particular bull thundered in and gored the lioness, throwing her in the air.

Immediately, all of the bulls encircled the wounded lioness, threw her once more and surrounded her, ready to storm her again if she rose.

My stomach was reacting to this spectacle, along with my weakened knees. Such a magnificent predator destroyed by these rogue buffalo. Another lioness came to defend the wounded lioness and the buffalo backed away slightly.

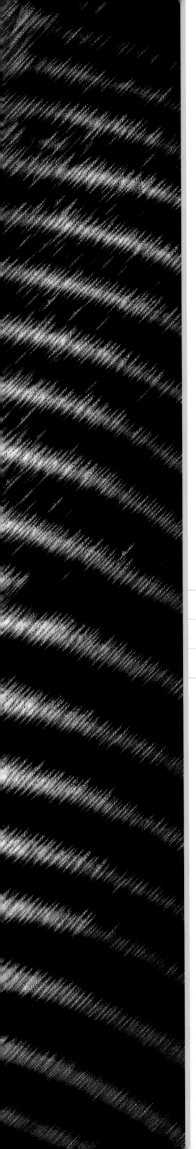

Some minutes later all buffalo departed. The buffalo that did the goring had a two-inch by one-inch-deep chunk of flesh missing from his nose, blood all over his horns and one eye swollen shut.

Some minutes passed and, amazingly, the lioness inched herself upright and walked off to lie in the shade. You could see her leg was badly injured, otherwise no external injuries showed. She was horribly pummeled and we may not know her fate for some time to come.

JOURNAL ENTRY - NGORONGORO CRATER

The next day we returned to locate the gored lioness and check on her condition. As we neared the site, no animals were visible. All we could observe was a patch of grass, about fifty feet across, that was laid flat. As we walked about the site, we found the lioness in the middle of the leveled grasses.

Everywhere were the tracks of buffalo, and what remained of the lioness was absolutely, completely flattened. Every one of her bones had to have been broken.

We suspect the buffalos returned to the dead, or dying, lioness and crushed her into the ground with the bosses of their horns until their passion was vented.

We have noticed several buffalo with their tails missing. Our guide tells us lions often seek initial control of a potential buffalo prey by taking hold of its tail. In ensuing battles, the tails are often severed by the predators. Lions and buffalo are archenemies; this time it was the buffalo that came out on the living end.

A bull cape buffalo is one of the most temperamental animals in Africa.

JOURNAL ENTRY - NGORONGORO CRATER

Moved to Ndutu. There are wildebeest and wildebeest kills all over the place. A lion with a kill, a hyena at a kill surrounded by vultures and vultures on other dead wildebeest in varying states of being consumed.

Photographed a dung beetle rolling a dung ball. Really neat.

I enjoy seeing things I've only read about in past years.

Every day another childhood vision comes true.

JOURNAL ENTRY - NDUTU

I wonder what the rest of the world is doing today? We're in the middle of the Serengeti with a multiple-mile-long line of wildebeest stretching out into the distance before us. Without an aircraft, it's virtually impossible to get decent photos of the masses across the landscape. From the ground all one sees is the front line of animals; all the animals in the background distance are obscured by the forward animals.

Flies are everywhere and they're landing all over us, seeking moisture from around our mouths and eyes. They become so persistent one must continually cover one's food and drink lest the flies cover it almost immediately. When the herd comes, so come the flies.

JOURNAL ENTRY

After all yesterday's rain, this morning dawned clear and damp. It was a good morning photographically, too. I photographed six rhinos, a rosy-breasted longclaw, lions being chased by a rhino, a waterbuck and army ants. Army ants crossing a road created a tunnel of living bodies through which the other ants passed.

Notice the fuzzy-topped ears on this locomotive-sized black rhino.

JOURNAL ENTRY
NDUTU

The rains ended this afternoon. Off we went sliding over the plains, taking photographs of dung beetles; they were having a heyday with the rain-softened dung and earth.

JOURNAL ENTRY
LAKE MANYARA

Cicadas fill the air with their ceaseless whirring. I enjoy this life on the road; the high moments really stick in one's mind. So hot and humid, still a blazing sun at 5 p.m.

JOURNAL ENTRY

Photographed a wildebeest giving birth.

We came at the end of a multiple birthing session, and the last wildebeest didn't cooperate for photographs but we did get to see the birth.

Photographing is frustrating at times; this trip has had many such moments. But that's it—the moment—trying to capture one fleeting moment at its special time. Those elusive moments keep a photographer going.

Still wet from birth, a wobbly newborn wildebeest calf struggles to take its first steps. Cow and calf will imprint upon each other to recognize scent and sound among hundreds of others in a herd.

*"Its quite lush here at the Mara
with recent rains."*

JOURNAL ENTRY
MASAI MARA

*I photographed an impala
scenting a bush and a vulture
pecking at an expired
Thomson's gazelle's nape and skull.*

It's quite lush here at the Mara with recent rains.

JOURNAL ENTRY

It was a slow, easy afternoon until we got into tsetse fly country and received several bites. Their bite is like a needle slowly being pressed through the skin.

Gratefully there was a torrential rain, an unrelenting downpour, that cleared them away. Last night, the deluge kept me awake until the torrent changed to pattering drops on the tent. Only then did I drift off with one of my favorite noises. The rain pattering on my tent made for my best sleep since arriving.

Of course, rainy weather also makes for difficult or impossible driving in many places.

Today the muffler on the Land Rover came apart, so it now sounds like a tractor and all the game dislikes the noise. So do I.

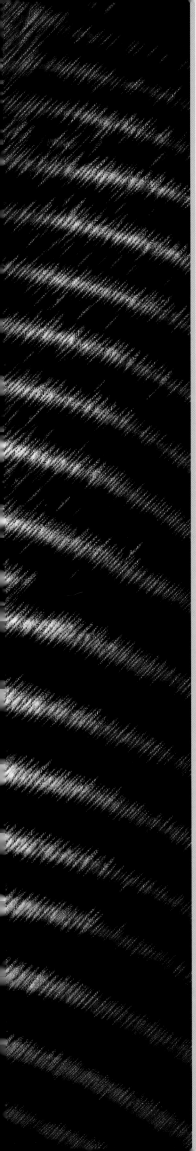

JOURNAL ENTRY

An exceptionally boring morning. Even so, the afternoon was exceptionally good photographically—we saw lions and more lions. The lions killed an adult and baby warthog before the sky opened up for more torrential rains.

The lions gathered into a sodden clump, then groomed, played, stalked and posed for 23 rolls of film.

JOURNAL ENTRY

I'm sitting on the toilet looking at an African killer bee on the screen door. The bee is quite large, otherwise I might squash it into these pages to show the people at home.

I exposed only two rolls of film this morning. We found bat-eared foxes but they wouldn't tolerate our tractor-sounding presence.

We heard reports of sixteen wild dogs in the area. My, my, I would like a photo session with them.

Just as this journal might be a wish book, we ran into the wild dogs— all sixteen of them, and we had an afternoon shoot of the pack but no kill. Nice portraits, greeting and running. Dare I wish for cheetah photos and leopard?

Overleaf: Wild dogs are among the most efficient hunters in Africa.

*". . . the afternoon was exceptionally good
photographically, lions and more lions."*

JOURNAL ENTRY - LAKE NAIVASHA

Rose this morning to a clear but hazy dawn. Thousands of flamingos, cacophonous sounds. We took the edge of the greatly receded Lake Nakuru for our photography. Flamingos are frustrating to photograph. They continually keep out of range and one can't follow them because of the lake's muck.

There's an interesting, terribly loud whining fly about the lake. Whine, whine, a single fly sounds like a dozen.

JOURNAL ENTRY
THE ABERDARE MOUNTAINS

A forested high-altitude woodland. It's going to be cold tonight; the sun has just set and we're huddled about the fire. Mount Kenya is off on the hazy east horizon.

JOURNAL ENTRY

Today, I've taken my best photos of warthog; you could see the color of his eyes and the hairs standing out on his body. I took my first photos of a Sykes monkey (also known as the blue monkey).

JOURNAL ENTRY

It's a gorgeous early sunrise and we're headed to the moorlands. Higher and higher, colder and colder as we climb above 11,000 feet. Rosewood trees, waterfalls, bamboo and so much tembo (elephant) sign. On our return it begins to rain, then pour, and the Land Rover slips and slides and spins.

As this chameleon moves across a branch with a swaying, fluttering walk, it mimics a leaf or foliage to increase its chance for survival.

Overleaf: The sound of startled flamingos can be nearly deafening.

55

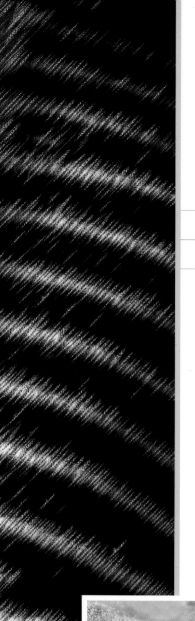

JOURNAL ENTRY - SAMBURU

I awoke at 4 a.m. to the sounds of elephants outside my tent.

I couldn't go back to sleep with all the rumbling, ripping of branches, farting and crashing from the elephants.

Then we broke camp to head toward northern Kenya—where desert life abounds.

We shivered our Land Rover over a 9,000-foot shoulder of Mt. Kenya to drop into the intense, frying midday heat in Samburu. There we had a flat tire. We forgot to tighten the tire nuts and the wheel almost fell off while driving.

The Land Rover's starter is just about shot, that is, short-ed out. The vehicle almost won't start when the engine is hot, and it is hot here. Ninety-plus degrees Farenheit in the shade and human skin in the equatorial sun burns in about fifteen minutes.

Play-jousting is one of the many forms of elephant interaction that includes touching, smelling and verbally communicating.

Impalas are always alert to their surroundings for possible danger.

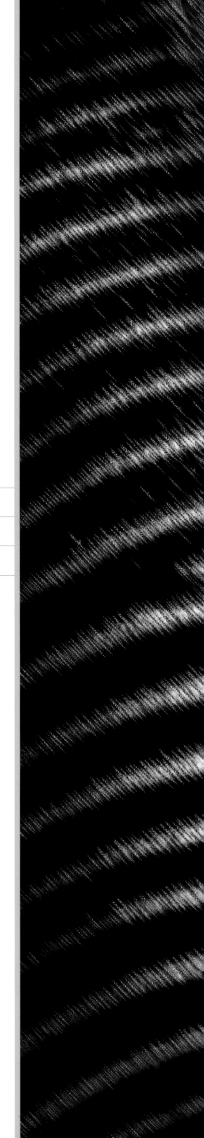

JOURNAL ENTRY

Earlier a baboon troop was at the river playing, swinging on vines and drinking in the river. A gray-headed kingfisher is all about camp, and the ever-present peering natives are across the river.

JOURNAL ENTRY

Warm days with cool nights for sleeping. A very frustrating morning for photography, a day when all the timing is off and any hesitation causes a missed shot. A photographer misses more pictures than he or she secures.

JOURNAL ENTRY - SHABA

Today is my last full day in the bush for this trip.

This morning I want to see the sunrise and take a few scenics in the gorge. I just want to sit back, enjoy the drive and say farewell to Africa without a camera in my face.

Being witness to an active lion pride, lions and lionesses playing, hunting and caring is a joy. Or to witness the speed of a cheetah or the impressive synchronized motion of a pack of wild dogs on the move.

I soak it all in because I don't know if, or when, I'll be back, perhaps never.

I've been here three times and I've marveled at the wilds and in so doing can recall the fact that I've been to Africa in my lifetime.

I've felt the winds, rains and sounds—those myriad voices in the night. I've fulfilled a childhood dream, maybe *the* childhood dream.

I'm thankful.

Caught in the final act of preening, a gray-headed kingfisher yawns and stretches its wings on a thorny perch of acacia branches. This species of kingfisher doesn't actually fish, but rather feeds on insects, grasshoppers and small lizards.

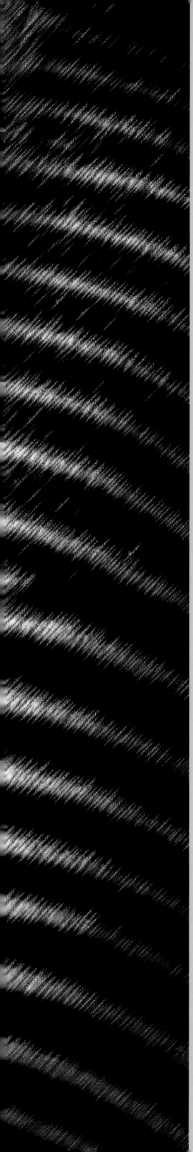

JOURNAL ENTRY - NAIROBI

Elephants are right- and left-brained just as we are. They use their trunks in a certain direction and favor one tusk over another as a right- or left-handed person would. Family groups, play and dominance acts, finding food, plus tool use are all behavior facets of humans not separate from other creatures.

Last evening we had a wonderful drive to Braguine Ridge; the wind was blowing hot dragon's breath and the sun lingered as it set.

On the return we encountered dozens of elephants at a spring, mud-bathing and drinking.

It all appeared primeval. All the way back to camp I rode in the open air atop the Land Rover.

So we bumped through the dust all the way to Nairobi. With dust-encrusted hair, we are out of the bush.

JOURNAL ENTRY

Returning to East Africa, after an absence of nine years, I wondered what I would find, what would have changed, whether the game would be as abundant as I previously thought and whether the visions from the past would be disappointed at the future.

Kenya is now 30 million people. Worthwhile wildlife areas include Ndutu in the Serengeti, Masai Mara, Tarangire and several private ranches.

Gone is the most wonderful game experience of all—Ngorongoro Crater. No longer is overnight camping allowed within the crater, nor can one drive off-road to photograph an animal as it goes about its business. At one time, perhaps, there was no better experience than to camp under a strangler fig tree, listen to tree hyraxes shriek in the night and have lions walk into the campsite to drink water from a spigot.

Notice the pale swolen tick on the eye of this large male bull elephant in the Ngorongoro Crater.

JOURNAL ENTRY

But back to Masai Mara, where I sit today. And I'm pleased to realize some things stay the same. The hyena still *churrups* its call across the night, lilac-breasted rollers still adorn the tops of low snaggled trees, wildebeest and zebra still follow their trails over grasslands.

The pieces of wildlife seem to be here, some quite literally, like the cape buffalo skull and the skull plates of impalas and gazelles, myriad vertebrae, leg bones and pieces of horn that litter the grasses.

Masai still over-graze their cattle and goats

and hope to sell their beadwork or have you buy

the rights to take their photograph.

JOURNAL ENTRY

Thunder and rain this afternoon, just like anywhere else in summer. In Kenya, they have the dry season and the rains, both a short rainy season in November and the long rains of April and May. Rain, on expectant afternoons, has a distinct lovely musky smell falling through the dusty, charged air and snuffing onto the dry grass and road tracks.

One has to be philosophical when one travels, and it would serve me well even in life, for as I travel, some days are good for photography, and others are rainy.

So, the rain allows me to favor attention on my writing, and to watch and listen to the bird song and insects.

When you look out over the horizon, it appears there is nothing to see. In reality, there may be hundreds of eyes watching you . . . like these zebras moving across the plains.

Overleaf: Gray crowned cranes take flight with a cacophonous call that sounds like a flock of geese.

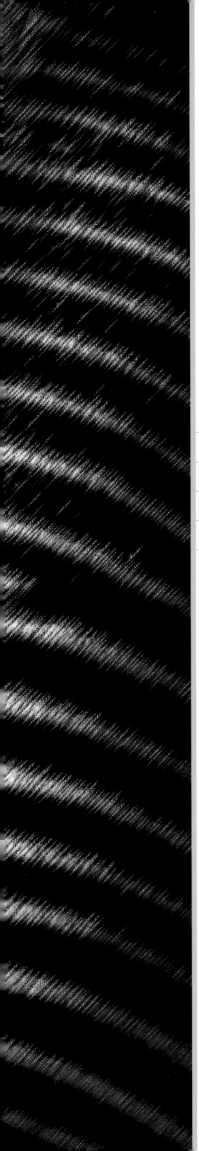

JOURNAL ENTRY

On our first drive out onto the plains, we're watching a family of cheetah sitting atop an old termite mound—a mother cheetah and her two young. We are close enough to occasionally hear these beautiful big cats purring; they're not too concerned with our presence.

Once young male cheetahs leave their mother, they will venture out on their own but stay together as hunting siblings.

Young female cheetahs stay with their mother longer than their male siblings. But once departed, they go their separate ways. The average age of cheetahs venturing on their own is around eighteen months.

Last night, when we went to bed, there were about two dozen hippopotamuses lazily floating in the Mara River alongside our camp. They were splashing, bellowing and snorting in a jolly sort of tone. The hippopotamuses are a familiar sight at this bend in the Mara River.

A hyena was scouting about camp, letting out repeated whoo-ooops.

Bush babies were coming down from their day roost, prancing across the roof of our tent, pitter-patter-patter.

I thought the strange, unfamiliar noises would keep me wide-eyed awake, but I had no trouble falling asleep.

Fading rays of golden sun complement the colors and markings of this cheetah's sleek coat.

JOURNAL ENTRY

Death. So life can prosper. It's a paradox that enthralls people about the African bush.

A newborn Thomson's gazelle was killed by a roving troop of baboons. A dominant male seized the motionless gazelle and trotted off to the perimeter with postures of threat toward any baboon that ventured near. In the end, the feeding male baboon was completely encircled by other males patiently waiting for a scrap to fall, or for the dominant male to have his fill and abandon the remains to the next strongest baboon in line.

Further down the pecking order, the smaller baboons were ignoring the whole hubbub, while they continued their normal breakfast of grass and forbs.

Nowhere on earth do I know of so many large mammals and birds living and dying on such a spectacular stage.

One minute there's a cantankerous cape buffalo bull with powerful eyes staring from inside a deep thicket. The next moment there's a new-born Thomson's gazelle trying out the spring in its new legs as it trots alongside mother. And the next moment zebras and wildebeest are crashing headlong over the plains with lions in dangerous pursuit.

The "big five," the grand slam of past trophy hunters, are here—rhinoceros, elephant, lion, buffalo, leopard. The good news is there hasn't been a black rhino poached in Kenya during the 1990s. Elephants are increasing since the world-wide ban on ivory. Lions are people's favorite African animal and they will survive on that fact alone. Buffalo were never threatened on a large scale by humans and the secretive leopard stays out of harm's way, surviving where habitat provides necessary cover and prey species.

I don't have a favorite animal of the big five—they're all so impressive. But the lilac-breasted roller is my favored bird; it is a resplendent flying rainbow of color.

During courtship and claiming of its territory, the lilac-breasted roller will roll over in flight displaying purples and blues for all to see.

JOURNAL ENTRY

It's only 10:30 a.m. and already I've identified twenty-three birds!

We proceeded over a hill into a thicket of bushes. In a small clearing of grass, there lay a huge male cape buffalo. We immediately stopped to judge his reaction to us.

After a time, we inched our way a little closer. That was close enough; he stood up, his nostrils trying to catch our scent.

He knew the safari vehicle, as I'm sure he's seen many, and once again laid his heavy body back into the grass.

We stayed with the buffalo for a long time, as this wasn't typical buffalo behavior. It's more normal to see their rear end as the buffalo is running for cover. Eventually this one rose up and walked slowly away— only looking back to give us one short glance, one that said, "You're lucky to have found me on a good day."

There's a symbiotic companionship between the Oxpecker and the cape buffalo. Rarely do you see one without the other.

Baboons often display human gestures. This young olive baboon is sucking its thumb.

JOURNAL ENTRY

We came upon two secretary birds. We repeatedly attempted to position the vehicle for the best light and composition, while also watching for ruts and termite mounds, and trying to predict the bird's next movements. Every effort was thwarted by the birds changing their travel direction. On some days, all this maneuvering can go perfectly; this was not one of those days.

We returned to the same place where we'd found a weak male lion yesterday. The lion was nowhere to be seen. He had either summoned the strength to scrounge a meal or had secluded himself in deep brush where, perhaps, he is dead or dying. I was hoping for the first option to have happened. It is a sad sight to see a starving, sick lion. When I think of a lion, I can only conjure up a noble, strong, well-muscled image. But this is reality in Africa.

Driving farther we came upon an extended family of olive baboons. The baboons paid us little attention. This was a large clan of all age groups. We decided to have our picnic breakfast here.

One of three large males was feeding
on a freshly killed newborn gazelle.

The other two males were keeping a close watch at a safe distance, picking up fallen scraps and eating the grass that had been bloodied by the gazelle's carcass. There was no fighting or yelling, just the silent understanding of hierarchy.

The feeding baboon would carry his gazelle about twenty feet away, then pause, pick off a few tidbits, then go another twenty feet distant, ever moving. Eventually, he ended up in thick underbrush and passed out of our sight along with the two attending males. I proceeded to pick at my breakfast of fruit and breads, but, h'mm . . . I wasn't feeling so hungry anymore.

Top: Secretary birds are often found in burned areas searching for snakes and insects. It will grab a snake with its feet, shaking the snake to death.

Bottom: This large male olive baboon stalked and killed a newborn Thompson's gazelle for its breakfast.

Overleaf: A black-and-white colobus monkey snoozes in the upper canopy shade of an acacia fever tree.

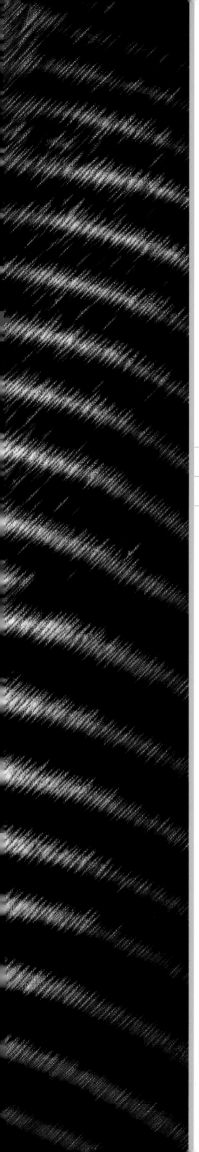

JOURNAL ENTRY

I wondered where all the vultures had gone. Nary a vulture has been seen in the sky all morning. That's because they were all walking through the grasses following a spotted hyena dragging a dead topi. We found them all today.

Whenever the hyena would move the carcass, the vultures would rush to that place to consume dropped topi pieces.

There must have been two hundred vultures walking in this group.

One of the reasons Africa is so predictably spectacular is that each time you drive onto the veldt you see a multitude of wildlife species; you always have multiple wildlife encounters.

We, as humans, are only one of the cultures that inhabit the earth. Indeed, with all the mammals, birds and insects, we have much to learn about our fellow natural citizens. We tend to focus on our species, believing we're the end-all in species evolution, but I don't think so.

We measure other beings against our strengths—how can any creature win with our biased test? Let these other creatures prepare the test and see how we humans fare.

If we were tested one on one, we'd be slower than almost any creature on the African plain; most of the animals would eat us for dinner. We can't see, smell or hear as well as the majority of animals. Our reflexes are poorer, so where would we end up in this "creature test"?

*"We were surrounded, enclosed by elephants.
We could have become an elephant sandwich . . . "*

JOURNAL ENTRY

We didn't get far from camp when we saw silhouettes of elephants walking slowly, single-file across the skyline. It is one of the images of Africa that will remain forever fixed in my memory.

The elephant family we watched consisted of five members, the matriarch, her newest born and an older daughter, along with one other mother (perhaps an aunt or sister) with her teenage daughter. They were moving within an acacia woods, headed in the direction of the swamp where the grass grows lush and tasty.

The youngest was just able to walk under its mother's belly.

All the elders were constantly keeping one eye on us, their other eye on the baby. A number of times, the baby ventured out past the protective crib of adults to mock-charge our vehicle, quickly turning around and rushing back toward mother. Another time, it came curiously forward, waving its trunk in an effort to smell what we were.

Farther across the savanna, another family of elephants started toward our group and behind them were more elephants! Before long we counted forty elephants. We were surrounded, enclosed by elephants. We could have become an elephant sandwich, but the moment didn't last. Good thing, because my heart was beating out of my chest.

I was feeling very small and vulnerable, which I was at that moment.

One cannot approach elephants too close, or too fast. It's best for you to let the elephant, or any wild animal for that matter, come to you by its own choice.

JOURNAL ENTRY

The adult elephants were tearing apart full-grown acacia trees, limb by limb.

They would tear off whole acacia branches with their powerful trunks and tusks, then feed on the leaves and branches, complete with thorns.

Elephants with larger tusks sometimes wedged their tusks in the crotch of an acacia tree. Comfortable enough, the elephants would then swing their long trunk over their tusks and proceed to rest, the weight of the elephants' head, trunk and tusks being supported by the acacia tree.

The elephants' ears would move slightly, the eyes would never close completely, the tip of the trunk would twitch once in a while. An elephant never seems to fall completely asleep, or to lie down for that matter.

In every direction there was life—impalas, gazelles, wildebeests, ostriches, buffalo, hyenas and lions! We spotted the lions thanks to numerous vultures soaring high above the big cats.

There were five lionesses and one big male lion, along with eight cubs of varying ages, all of them napping.

I'm realizing napping is one of the things lions do best. Their bellies were full and content.

No longer do you see the "big tuskers" of the past.

The adult male seems to be in charge . . .

Overleaf: But the activity of these young cubs forces him to abandon the only shade for miles.

"This was a peculiar first sighting for me."

All of the lions were trying to huddle in the shade of a very small tree. Looking around, we didn't see another tree for a very long distance. They were panting, leaning into one another, squeezing into every inch of shadow or shade. One small cub was restless, climbing over the backs, bellies and heads of its family. One lioness lifted her head and snarled at the little one, then pinched the cub's cheek skin between her massive teeth—ouch!

Driving back toward camp, we came upon a family of warthogs grazing grass. This was a peculiar first sighting for me.

If you got down on your hands and knees, you would know how a warthog walks.

Although, if you bent to your elbows while you were down there, then you would know how it feels to feed like a warthog. All across the grassland they are walking on their knees with elbows bent to reach the tender grass and roots with less effort.

Warthogs are born with white whiskers to resemble the tusks which will eventually grow in the whiskers' place. If they run in fear, their tail stands straight up like an antenna. When they reach their excavated holes in the ground, they back themselves into the hole, keeping their formidable tusks facing outward.

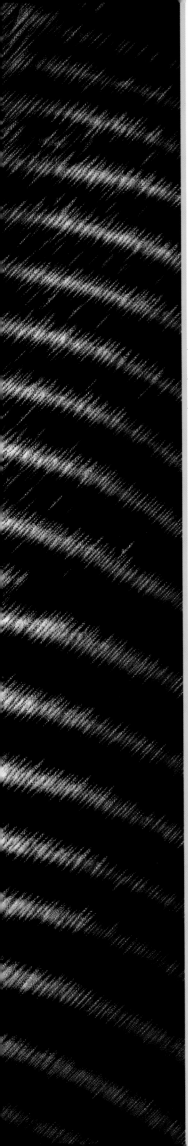

JOURNAL ENTRY

Each morning we head in a slightly different direction, with each day offering a different landscape. We stopped on the crest of a hill, looking over thousands of acres, and saw no civilization. What a wonderful feeling.

We noticed movement ahead in the short grasses, three hyenas, trotting at a steady pace. Trotting as if they knew exactly where they were going.

The wind was carrying a scent to the hyena's nose and we were just as curious to follow.

Driving over the hill, the landscape changed from grassland to jagged, protruding lava rock. Like a moonscape, there was no road or trail to be seen.

The hyenas had led us to a lion kill. There were four young male lions and not much left of a wildebeest. They had made the kill in early morning. One of the lions was still feeding on the skull, trying to tear a portion of the hide away from the neck. As he scraped his teeth against the skull bone, the sound was that of chewing on hard gristle. When the lion had his fill, he got up, stretched his legs and took off to join the other lions in the shade.

Leftover wildebeest. I was waiting for our driver to ask if we wanted to have our picnic breakfast here. He seems to have a knack for breaking out our meal while watching the tail end (literally) of someone else's meal. I am getting used to the idea of everyone having a full belly at the same time.

Now the waiting hyenas knew it was safe to move in and they wasted no time. They hadn't come trotting all this way for nothing.

We broke out the picnic boxes and had our breakfast. At least we were upwind.

Top: A spotted hyena stands guard over the skull plate of a Thompson's gazelle in a dew-covered landscape.

Bottom: Often the gray crowned crane is found following a herd of grazing animals that are stirring up insects upon which the cranes feed.

JOURNAL ENTRY

An African safari is a sensory overload.

By the time several days pass, repeated morning and afternoon photo drives overwhelm the mind. Let me give you an example: this afternoon we drove for three hours, spending time photographing most of the game animals we encountered.

A partial listing of what we saw follows: two beautiful male lions yawning and napping, two dozen hippopotamuses basking on river's edge with a day-old baby, two troops of baboons, white-backed vulture, lilac-breasted roller, robin chat, black-bellied bustard, little bee-eaters, multiple hyenas, thirty elephants, gray crowned crane, black-chested harrier eagle, eland, Egyptian geese, red-billed hornbill, and a banded mongoose, dwarf mongoose, aardwolf, pied kingfisher, wattled plover, spotted barbet, gray-crowned shrike, cape buffalo, topi, sunbird, woolly-necked stork, maribou stork, caracal (a beautiful tawny, tuft-eared cat), giraffe, hamerkop, auger buzzard, African fish eagle, kestrel, gray-headed kingfisher, red-billed oxpecker and the too-numerous-to-count impala, zebra, wildebeest, Thomson's and Grant's gazelles.

Constantly traveling in packs of up to forty, banded mongooses communicate in a chitter-chatter.

The distinctly patterned reticulated giraffe is not as widely distributed as its cousin, the Masai giraffe.

Overleaf: Usually quiet, yellow-billed storks can become very noisy when protecting a nest.

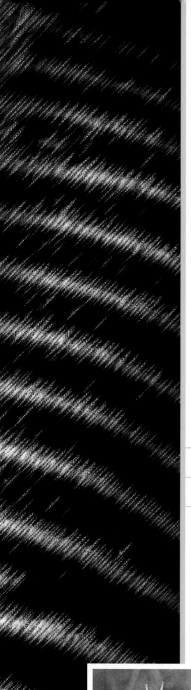

JOURNAL ENTRY

After two days of soaking rains, the ground became saturated and soft enough to trigger a massive, incredulous termite flowering. Once night covered the plains winged termites filled the air around every outdoor light. Their gossamer three-inch wingspan glistened in the shine.

Several hours later, I walked to see acres of shed wings littering the ground. The termites bite off their wings and begin to crawl off looking for a suitable piece of ground where they can begin excavating a nest site.

It is the "short rains," the time when rain comes for a period of weeks, as contrasted to the "long rains," which last for months.

Most days are cloudy and, very often,

in the late afternoon, the sky begins to cry rain.

The birds fly to dry shelter, the cats abhor rain and also look for cover, while the ungulates carry on or lie on the savanna as if there is nothing they can do but accept the rain, which is also true. Rains are very good for the antelope—the grasses will thrive.

The large southern ground-hornbill uses its bill for digging up and tossing insects into its mouth.

A superb hunter, the tawny eagle can easily handle killing a mongoose, newborn gazelles and even other large birds.

JOURNAL ENTRY

A leopard is always a special sighting. Today there were two leopards together, a mother and her nine-month-old daughter. The mother had killed a male Thomson's gazelle and dragged it to and up the lone tree on the veldt. Mother leopard carried the gazelle into the treetop to avoid its being stolen by a wandering pride of lions or hyenas. There, hidden up high, the leopards consumed their meal.

Lightning suddenly struck the nearby escarpment that backs up along the Mara River on this sunny day. Just as quickly a serpentlike thunderhead of cloud rushed over the nestling hills and, in one swoop, engulfed the hills and our camp in torrential rains. Now, two hours later, the sky is dusky gray and rains are raising the Mara River's muddy waters. I can hear the hippos grunting and bellowing—what do the hippos think of this rain, especially the tiny newborns I saw along the river yesterday?

So many unanswered questions. What are the dark moths that lay their eggs on the horns of skulls so their larvae can consume the horn material? What is the name of the tree with the perfectly forked branches that the leopard hangs its gazelle in? Why does an elephant put its trunk into another elephant's mouth?

Every day I have more unanswered questions, but I also discover answers. The hyena's droppings are gray-white because they eat so many bones, eagles eat termites, tree hyrax have a banshee wail all out of proportion to their small size, eland have a high "bucking bronco" jump when alarmed, hippos exude a skin oil-sweat that helps prevent sunburn and also serves as an antibiotic to the many cuts they inflict upon each other, wildebeest have split hooves, zebras don't, a hyena will eat a lion, but a lion won't eat a hyena.

Top: Leopards will haul their kills high up into trees, out of other predators' reach, before beginning to feed. This leopard dines on a Grant's gazelle, an antelope that can weigh up to 180 pounds!

Bottom: Common eland are the largest—and slowest—member of the antelope family. These two males are watching a pride of sleeping lions in the distance.

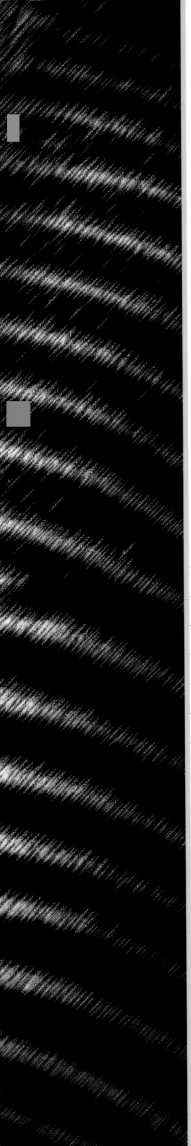

JOURNAL ENTRY

Here stands a baby topi without a mother to be seen, in the middle of a black, burned-out field—a "blue plate special."

Later, a huge pride of lions, twenty cubs and eight lionesses, are walking somewhere down a dirt road. They're returning to a small wooded area they have claimed as their own. The small forest provides shade and cover, and also serves as a nursery of sorts.

Prior to seeing these lions, we drove past a fresh kill site in trodden grass. A lower leg, a portion of a rib cage and the skull of a zebra were all that remained. The lions had fed early this morning and were returning to their woods to snooze.

The young, little lions were in a playful mood, boxing each other, stalking each other and using tree trunks for scratching posts.

Other sightings this morning were a male impala with a rear broken leg, a bat-eared fox and young in their den, a giraffe and her young feeding on acacia trees, four curious jackals (two adult, two young), a female leopard and young with the remains of a Thomson's gazelle hanging in a tree, an agama lizard and a European bee-eater.

It's afternoon and there is solid rain falling outside our tent. Pools of water are collecting wherever the terrain is flat. The season of short rains leaves both photographer and driver questioning each other, "Should we go looking for photographs or not?"

Our camp is located on the banks of the Mara River. We can watch the river's water level rising from the recent rain. The two dozen hippos occupying this stretch of river just bob and float by us.

Top: Eternally nervous to the presence of predators, bat-eared foxes spend the day close to the safety of their dens.

Bottom: Lions seem tolerant to sharing a kill with the black-backed jackal, which quickly darts in to snatch a morsel of food, then moves off a safe distance before feeding.

JOURNAL ENTRY

In the evening, all the hippos leave the river for its banks to feed on grasses up to three kilometers away. In the early morning, we can often see a group of hippos lying on the opposite shore, slowly stirring each other into waking. There are deep pathways the hippos have created along the riverbanks where they move in and out of the river.

Hippopotamuses are quite vocal throughout the day and, especially, during the evening. I've grown accustomed to falling asleep to the sounds of the hippos. I wonder how to describe the sounds of a hippo. They remind me of a laughing tuba. It's a very deep, bass rumbling—sometimes a snort or even a snorting laugh.

They spend unbelievable amounts of time submerged in the water; their body is not so heavy in the water and they're safer from predators.

Hippo heaven. Water cool and deep enough to pass the midday heat, and vegetation tasty enough to snack upon between naps.

A rare sight—a newborn hippopotamus baby is zealously guarded and cared for by its mother in these early days of life.

JOURNAL ENTRY

Predators and prey, that's Africa. Nothing goes to waste in the scheme of survival here. Before I had witnessed an actual kill happening, I wasn't sure how sensitive I'd be to the tearing and ripping of flesh.

But what I've seen has helped me to understand the symbiotic roles of predator and prey. A zebra will be killed in the early hours of morning, and by sunset, you can hardly tell anything has happened at the kill site, even the bones are carried away. We notice partial skulls and shards of bones lying in the short grasses—even these are inhabited by beetles and moths that eventually help them back into the soil that nourishes the grasses that feed the zebra.

When I do witness some animal being taken down by a predator,
I try to keep in mind this cycle of life.

This little bee-eater perches awaiting the next passing bug.

With legs built for speed and jumping, this male impala runs with great agility.

JOURNAL ENTRY

A baby male elephant, shorter but much heavier than I, was charging our vehicle. Pulling up short, dirt flying, he trumpeted as if to say, "C'mon, Mom, let's take care of this threatening thing." Thankfully, the mother was content to feed on a nearby acacia tree.

Photographing elephants is serious business. Bull elephants weigh 11,000 pounds; our Land Rover weighs but 4,000. If the herd of elephants passes near the Land Rover, the sky diminishes, the air fills with elephant communication rumbles and sometimes with the trumpet of a charging baby troublemaker.

JOURNAL ENTRY

Roads are slick like grease from last night's rains. We began our drive this morning watching a family of elephants. It was the same herd we spent time photographing two days ago. The mother elephant is doing her job well by keeping herself between us and her baby.

The elephants are on the move this morning, twisting off a clump of grass with their trunks, then walking on.

A small herd of impala came running past the elephants as if being chased by a predator. We never saw the elephants move as quickly as we did just then. They immediately came together and formed a circle around the young. Tusks facing outward, ears flared out.

They stayed in this formation for a full ten minutes before spreading out again to continue feeding.

Top: An elephant's trunk is powerful enough to rip branches from a tree, yet dextrous enough to pluck fruit.

Bottom: Fleet of foot and able to go extended periods with little or no water, the Beisa oryx inhabits some of the drier areas of Africa. Both sexes grow long, spear-like horns.

Overleaf: An elephant family comprised of sisters, aunts and the matriarchal leader will stay together for life, if possible.

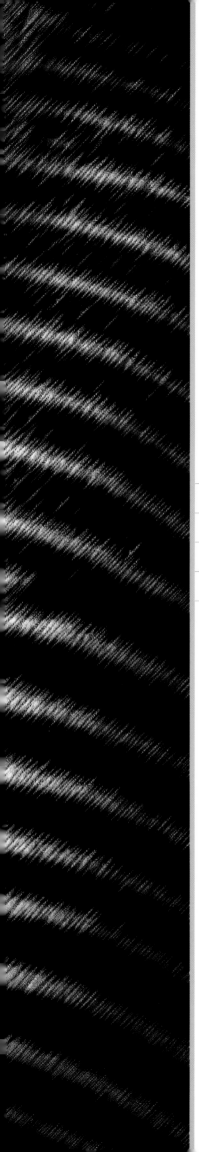

JOURNAL ENTRY

This afternoon, we discovered a female cheetah with two young; they were lounging in the tall grass under the shade of a tree. One of the young became restless, prodding its mother to move, to look for food. The rest of our evening was spent watching these cheetahs, until the sun had set and we needed to return to camp.

I had mixed emotions. Mixed emotions about man's interference with animals making their living, survival as it is.

I understand how portions of the money we spend in and around parks or reserves is "supposed" to benefit the animals and their habitat. I'd like to believe, perhaps naively, that this applies here in the Mara of Kenya, that this reserve would not be here were it not for the people who come to see the lions, elephants and other animals.

But while watching the cheetah and her two young trying to capture a gazelle, on three different attempts, only to be cut off by a safari vehicle or Masai walking through the herd of gazelle, I felt the conflicting emotions of humans overwhelming and encroaching upon the animals and their natural patterns of survival. We stayed at a distance watching the cheetahs and everyone around them. They never ate anything while we were there. Perhaps tomorrow.

JOURNAL ENTRY

Elephants, elephants, a trip for elephants. A large group of mothers and babies accompanied by a large bull walked at us in the grasses.

I sat low and watched the massive gray line approach. You know the feeling when a serious storm is heading your way; you never know if it will be violent or pass with a gentle rain. When these titans pass near, I'm very careful not to make sudden moves or noises. I'm not afraid, I'm just cautious and don't know what kind of day this elephant has been having.

Silently, they were upon me, twenty-nine in number, towering overhead, in front of me, on every side and soon all around me traveling en masse. As the mothers passed near, they would usher their babies to their side opposite me—the mother's body acting as a powerful shield toward any creature they don't wish to take a chance on trusting.

It seems difficult to look an elephant in the eye. There are so many distracting parts to an elephant—the moving trunk, the flapping ears, the tree-bole legs—and just looking up at a giant is intimidating. Even when I concentrate on looking at and into the eyes themselves, I can't read the workings of the immense brain. The elephant knows what it's feeling. For now that's enough for me.

Until I heard the breathing, rumbling and rustling of elephant hide on the brush, I always felt the distance in my relationship with pachyderms.

When an elephant smells me with extended trunk. When I have an acacia tree torn limb from limb and its leaves are blowing upon me. When I see the trust it takes for a mother to nurse her young so close to me I can hear the suckling. When all of this happens within a stone's throw of the Land Rover, then I know what intimacy is possible.

This baby elephant is testing its ability to intimidate with a bluff-charge. No matter the result, mother is nearby to back up its bluff if needed.

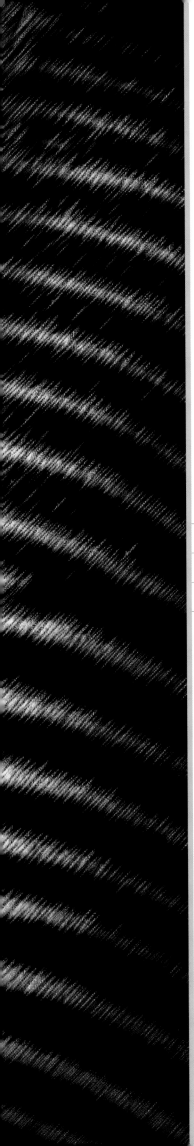

JOURNAL ENTRY

At a herd of grazing Thomson's gazelle, we spied three cheetahs advancing in a line. It was obvious they were hunting. Quickly we surveyed the gazelles for youngsters. There were two.

As soon as the main herd saw a cheetah, one female Tommy took her young and fled in the opposite direction.

The cheetah zeroed in on the remaining baby and began a run from many hundred yards distant. Closing in, the cheetah accelerated, coming dangerously close to touching the young gazelle. And then it was over. The little gazelle zigged, the cheetah zagged and came to an abrupt stop—out of wind.

What the little gazelle didn't know was that its escape path had taken it toward one of the grown cheetah cubs who initiated the second phase of the chase.

The end came in seconds. The third cheetah overtook the tired gazelle youngster and the second young cheetah grabbed another part of the gazelle in a tug-of-war.

Soon, their mother joined the grown youngsters and consumed the little gazelle in minutes.

Top: Diurnal hunters, cheetahs rely on their eyesight, stealth and speed for successful hunting.

Bottom: These siblings will soon leave their mother to hunt on their own.

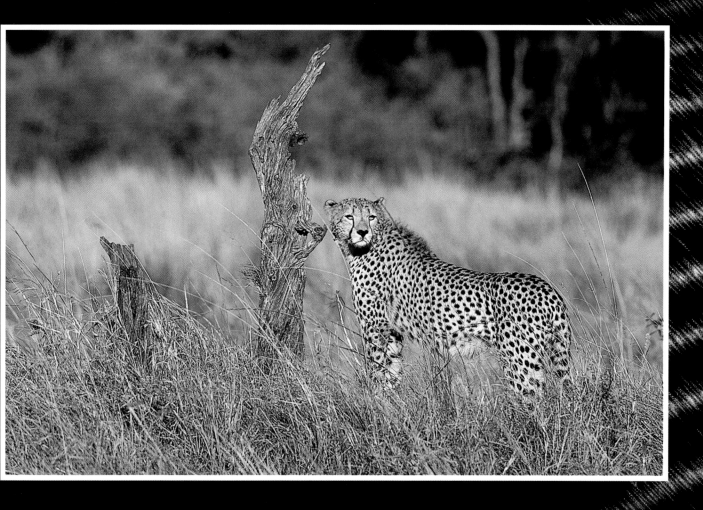

JOURNAL ENTRY

This morning we located a pride of lions at the same location we saw them last evening just as it became too dark to photograph. We were hoping they had made a kill and we could film them feeding. Instead, the lions were all lying prone, deep in catnaps, except for a restless cub crawling over two lionesses. We paused the vehicle when it was certain these lions were totally content to sleep.

Sparkles of sun ricochet in and off the droplets of dew and rain adorning the grasses and acacia trees. In the bright light of sunrise a line of elephants cross the horizon in silhouette. Stopping to let the elephants pass, barking zebras and nervous hyenas call upon the morning breeze.

Morning calm is deceptive as a lioness raises her head from tall grasses to survey her nearby domain.

Warthogs, some with tiny piglets, streak away with tails held erect like antennas. A topi has located the lioness, and uncertain of her intent, the topi stares and snorts.

This, in turn, makes nearby Thomson's gazelles and a few impalas do the same stare and snort routine, until caution sends all but the topi bounding for distant grazing. But it's shade the lion seeks; the heat of the day is beginning to grow too warm to hunt.

Elephants are also turning their direction to the shade of the river forest, their ears waving to dissipate their body heat while feeding and moving. Eighteen hours a day are spent filling those giant stomachs with plants.

A few dozen vultures begin riding the thermals, soaring in circles in search of a kill. They spy the remains of a Grant's gazelle high in a tree, a leopard's unfinished food cache. Maneuvering into and under branches, the vultures wrestle their breakfast while the leopard sleeps elsewhere.

Soon the sun is hot, and a pause takes place on the Serengeti. Animals sit out the midday heat. So do I.

Top: This lioness was but one of many that were napping unseen in the grasses.

Bottom: At the edge of a kill site, vultures patiently await their turn for what remains of a carcass.

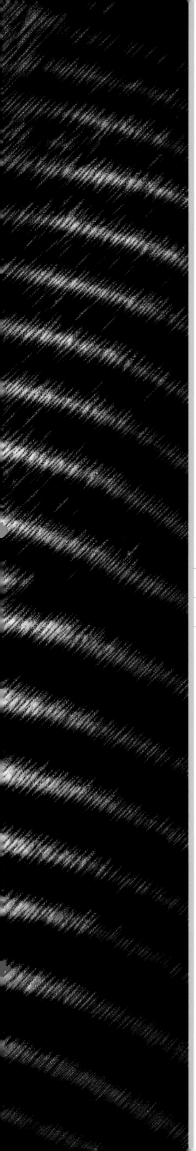

JOURNAL ENTRY

This morning we left camp a little earlier than usual in hopes of meeting up with a more active lion pride. We would check around the same area where we left the pride last night.

We found the lion pride . . . sleeping. Their stomachs were extended, obviously full from a late-night meal. They hardly lifted an eyelid when they heard the approach of our vehicle. The sun was still rising, so there was no need for them to hide in the shade of trees.

We counted seventeen cats; six were lionesses, the rest were cubs of various ages. We sat for a long time just watching them sleep. Occasionally young cubs would move about, trying to stir the other cubs, boxing with each other and generally making nuisances of themselves.

Everyone who comes to East Africa wants to see lions. The lions display an amazing level of tolerance toward people who want to be near them.

At times I feel ashamed to be part of the human race when I see what these animals must tolerate from us.

It's not the first time I have felt this way. I'm not guilt-free, for I've also come here to see the lions. I'm one of the Land Rovers that follows the animal. I'm one of the "foreigners" who have come to hear the lion roar, see the cheetah pursue and watch the elephant walk.

We try to keep a respectable distance when photographing. There are, however, certain situations when you find yourself close to animals by their choice. And that is enough to make your heart feel like jumping out of your chest with excitement.

Top: A large male lion drinks from a shrinking water hole after gorging himself upon a buffalo kill.

Bottom: Cubs soon learn to stay alert to danger. Even the youngest try to be ferocious.

116

JOURNAL ENTRY

On days when things aren't going well in your world or when you're feeling sorry for yourself, picture this . . .

You're a virile young male lion, your mane is fully grown but has yet to blacken with full maturity and you are roaming the countryside with a pretty young lioness looking for a place to begin a life together.

Your life is about to change in a big way because you have just noticed two large male lions, and they're coming your way.

Territorial possession becomes an issue between the newcomer and the mature males; after all, the virile young male has a female to impress.

The young male is strong, but fighting experience and sense of turf heavily favor the older lions. And so the newcomer is badly slashed and bitten. The elder lions show no mercy and the first light of day finds the young lion barely able to see, his face is badly torn, there are punctures about his neck and blood drains from his nose and mouth from internal hemorrhaging.

Some nomadic Masai dogs and cattle tenders have discovered this lion heaped in the middle of some thorn bush. It's not a pretty sight. As the day wears on more Masai come to see the fallen warrior, more dogs bark at the sunken lion and he must summon failing strength to even raise his head and open his eyes. Dying like this, there is no dignity.

The Masai grow bolder, approach closer. In late afternoon one Masai touches the lion with his foot and the lion can't turn his head. The life in his eyes is glowing low, he is paying for his trespass and vigor with his life.

Just prior to sunset, the life drains from the young male lion's eyes, his body relaxes; a Masai covers his body with acacia tree branches. So promising a future burning brightly and so quickly a life ended.

The next time you feel life is mistreating you, remember your life is not as bad as this lion's life was today.

The lion pride had already left on their dusk hunt by the time this male lion yawns himself awake before trailing after his pride.

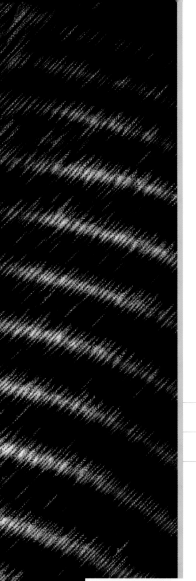

JOURNAL ENTRY

The wind blew all night long and faded to a cooling whisper by sunrise. Perhaps it is the swirling breezes that pass the scent of predators to the grass-eaters. All across the plains, with the new grasses greening, I can see animals moving with not a cat in sight. Antelopes and gazelles are celebrating this glorious morning with vigorous haphazard running, with directionless bursts of speed, apparently carrying on for the sheer pleasure of the moment. Death usually seems near; not today.

Watch the topi carefully; it stands, ever watching, atop nearby and distant mounds, elevated so it can see the distant miles.

The topi will tip you off to a predator's whereabouts, for it will stare exactly at the place the predator is. If I were an antelope, I would want to travel with a topi.

Both the male and female topi have horns. Here a calf adds mother's milk to its diet of grasses.

When you see a gathering of vultures in the treetops, you can be fairly certain a kill is nearby.

120

"They can smell their destination."

JOURNAL ENTRY

A head moving through the waist-high grasses. More motion, another head, then four, ten, then twenty, maybe thirty or more, all shoulder to shoulder and end to end. It's difficult to see in the long red oat grasses.

OK, they're waist high, now; they begin to look like antelope heads—they are antelope heads. Thomson's gazelles, but why in the long grass? They traditionally love the short-grass open plains where they can see great distances and flee danger before it draws nearer.

I've watched these gazelles approaching for at least a mile through these grasses.

Don't they know big cats sleep in tall grass? The gazelles know, that's why they're so nervous, traveling so close to one another and often jumping up on hind legs to get a better look around.

They can smell their destination. I wish them safe travels, as I wish the leopard good hunting.

JOURNAL ENTRY

Down a dusty road we could see a few giraffe heads peering over the treetops, watching our approach—at least I think they were watching us. It's difficult to tell if the giraffe is looking at you, or three miles past and above you.

The acacia trees get their shape by giraffes pruning the undersides as high as they can reach, resulting in the flat bottoms of trees.

Overleaf: Towering over the acacia trees they're feeding on, two Masai giraffes watch our Land Rover approach.

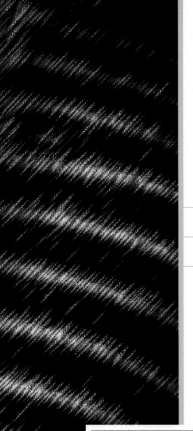

JOURNAL ENTRY

We drove upon two large male lions just finishing their morning zebra.

They were handsome males, just as one would envision a male lion in his prime—full mane shining golden with morning light.

Their bellies were full and they could barely stay awake long enough to watch a pair of jackals moving in for leftovers. We left them to their dreams of antelope.

We wanted to stop so we could glass the surrounding area, look for animals, take a short break.

After we had done all of this and even gone to visit a bush, we noticed a leopard looking down on us from the shade of a nearby treetop. This was the first time I saw a leopard.

The leopard had what remained of a Thomson's gazelle hanging in the branch where the cat straddled. We watched for some time, when immediately in front of us, this leopard's young suddenly came out of the grass.

I now knew that leopards spend much of their time in the trees, feeding, resting and watching. So, forever after, while driving, I spent a lot of time looking up, watching for that certain unmistakable outline.

A leopard feels comfortable looking out from the crotch of a large tree.

King of the plains, a male lion's life span will be shorter than that of the females. Always defending their territories against rival males, only the strongest survive.

JOURNAL ENTRY

I opened the door of the Land Rover and had walked only a step or two when the rock hyrax all squeaked their alarms. Our driver shouted, "Quick, get back in!" I turned to see a hyena running directly for me, at great speed.

The hyena had started its run from a patch of grasses approximately fifty yards distant. We hadn't seen it when we stopped. It had covered about half the distance by the time the rock hyrax and our driver had sounded the alarm.

Once I was back inside the Land Rover, the hyena cut its chase short. I suspect what happened was the animals view you differently apart from the vehicle.

The hyena must have interpreted my sudden appearance as prey being flushed out of the grasses by the vehicle. And when I disappeared—back into the safety of the Land Rover—the hyena saw its potential meal disappear.

Then we realized that this had been only one of six hyenas in the immediate area. For in a nearby depression on the ground, we saw many broken eggshells. It was a nest a male ostrich was still trying to protect. If there had only been one or two hyenas instead of six, he would have held his ground and protected the eggs and nest.

But the hyenas were many, too many, and he broke ground. The hyenas smashed the eggs by rolling them back and forth against one another. All of the eggs had broken except for one. The hyenas had this last egg twenty feet distant from the original nest site. They knew there was food inside and they kept trying to bite the egg.

When biting didn't work, they took the egg with their hind legs and kick-pawed the egg several feet through the air. They were hoping to break the egg, but their tactic wasn't working. Try as they might, the egg just continued to bounce and roll unbroken through the grasses.

Top: Both adult ostrich play an active part in raising their family. Here a male Somali ostrich leads his brood to cover.

Bottom: Still perplexed as to how to crack open a thick-shelled ostrich egg, a spotted hyena kicks, paws and attempts to bite open the egg.

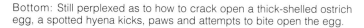

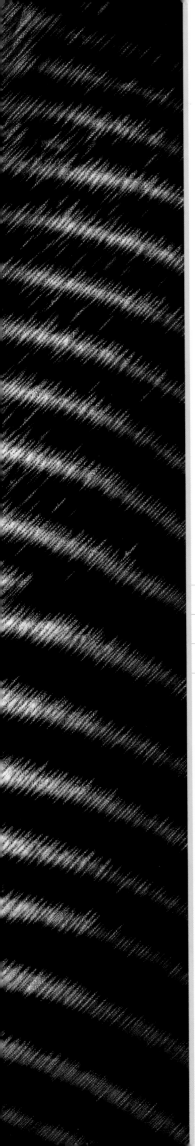

JOURNAL ENTRY

Not much daylight remained as we drove to where a female rhino had been reported. We spotted her from far away. She was out in open grasses. This was a very special sighting for all of us.

We learned from our guide that this was surely the daughter of a rhino that had been shot on Rhino Ridge. This rhino had survived her orphanage against all odds.

We looked closely with the binoculars; she appeared well fed with no obvious scars and her horn had grown to some length. She continued to browse on young acacia trees while we watched her until darkness blended all shapes into one.

The word was out. A rhino

had returned to the Mara.

For how long, no one knew.

It was interesting how fast the word spread. During all of our driving the next day, we never saw another vehicle. Everyone was looking for the rhino that had at long last wandered back to the Mara.

JOURNAL ENTRY

People often ask how I find all these animals doing the things they're doing in my photographs. Besides simply being "out there" with the animals in their habitat (actually "our" habitat), I look for a variety of signs and evidence.

First, I watch for any prey animal—antelope, zebra, gazelles and especially topis—looking intently in a particular direction. If these animals have been focusing their undivided attention at a specific piece of ground, chances are there are one or more big cats at the end of their stare.

Second, if there is a gathering of vultures, either in a group of trees, soaring over one place in the distance or, better yet, all gathered on the ground with a few jackals included, you've probably located a kill. If the vultures are perched in trees, odds are the predators are still feeding below the vultures and the vultures are patiently awaiting their turn. If the vultures are on the ground, the predator will have abandoned the kill after already feeding, or else the birds have found a natural death of an animal.

If you see white splotches all over a group of rocks and on the ground, there's a good chance of discovering a kill site. Upon closer inspection, you'll probably find many vulture feathers lost during squabbles at the carcass and from their preening afterward. The white splotches are vulture guano. There should be telltale bones or a skull nearby.

Baboons will telecast the closeness of a leopard
(their mortal enemy) by seeking the protective cover of trees
and raising an unholy ruckus of shrieks, thereby
lending credence to the term, "catcalls."

If hyenas find a leopard kill out in the open where the leopard can't take its meal up a tree, the hyenas will drive the cat away and take the prey.

Top: With a long prehensile tail used for balance and climbing trees, a male vervet monkey makes his way through the grasses searching for foods to satisfy his omnivorous diet.

Bottom: A leopard's coat is good camouflage in the tall grasses.

Overleaf: A slow shutter speed blurs this leopard with the remains of a Thomson's gazelle.

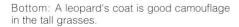

133

I also look for cheetahs on the tops of mounds where they are surveying the plains. I look in trees for dark shapes; these may be leopards resting on their kills (usually a gazelle) pinched in the fork of branches. Lions will be in the shade as soon as the sun begins to heat.

Sometimes, I have spied a young animal without a mother nearby. On the plains you can always locate its mother unless the young has been orphaned by the mother's death.

If the mother is gone, the young will be prey
for the next group of lions or hyenas that come along.

Sometimes you'll notice a shape in the distance that looks like a cheetah or a lion and when you raise your binoculars you see your cheetah or lion is, in reality, a rock or a tree stump shaped like a cat. I call those eye-foolers, cheetah rocks, lion (or whatever animal it was shaped into) stumps.

A blacksmith plover in grasses that ungulates have nipped off. The plover's voice serves as an early predator warning to surrounding animals.

Reflections of two yellow-billed storks mirror the sky and the stretching birds just prior to their taking flight.

JOURNAL ENTRY

Images of the Mara.

Huge flocks of flamingos
calmly feeding,
constantly murmuring.

The lone baby giraffe, not two weeks old (dried umbilical cord dangling), feeding quietly on acacia leaves, while on a hill, still in sight, the rib cage and leg bones of its mother lie among the rocks.

Newborn Thomson's gazelles standing on wobbly legs, only to pronk off like they have springs in their legs a short time later.

The tiniest baby hippo next to its gigantic mother on a stretch of the crocodile-infested Mara River.

Elephants surrounding the Land Rover, their stomachs rumbling, trunks smelling us, then using the same trunk to rip an acacia tree limb from limb.

Masai cattle, like visions of the American West, spread out on miles of grasslands.

Fire lilies blossom after the rains. Their petals reach skyward shaped and colored like flickering flames.

Early morning finds this large flock of flamingos bathing, preening and feeding in a shallow soda lake.

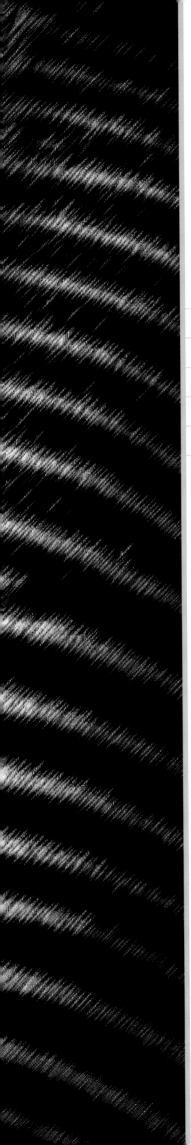

JOURNAL ENTRY

Near the Aitong Hills we came across a mother cheetah with three very young cubs. Around six weeks of age, cheetah cubs will venture out to hunt with their mother. Before that time, the mother keeps the cubs out of sight, hidden in the tall grasses.

We watched them moving through islands of bushes. The mother told the cubs to stay put as she moved ahead into thick grass. She zigzagged a couple of times in the grass and emerged with a hare firmly caught by the back of its neck. The small kittens never budged until their mother called to them.

The three youngsters wasted no time eating the tender hare. The mother took only two or three small bites, keeping watch for any danger to her vulnerable cubs.

When they were almost finished, a few white-backed vultures started wheeling overhead; one landed nearby, along with a tawny eagle. Had one of these been a martial eagle, the mother would have immediately moved her cubs to safety.

Even after the vultures arrived, the mother was more wary; vultures attract the attentions of other predators.

The cheetahs spent the next thirty minutes cleaning and grooming each other, before their catnap.

Top: The mother cheetah has just captured this African hare. She searches the area while calling out her hidden kittens to share her prize.

Bottom: After feeding, a young cheetah purrs while being groomed by its mother.

"The morning sun doesn't linger
at the horizon; instead it climbs straight up
in the equatorial sky."

JOURNAL ENTRY

As the pre-sunrise light barely brings the trees to shape against the sky, just as the slightest breeze pushes the cool mists along the ever-flowing Mara River and as the first robin-chat's song startles the ears, the elephants appear in a line across the horizon.

Black-headed herons and baboons depart their tree roosts overhanging the river where they spent the night in safety from their dangers.

Egyptian geese explode in flight from around a river bend, low to the water's surface, until alighting on a peninsula in the river.

The morning sun doesn't linger at the horizon; instead it climbs straight up in the equatorial sky. Only for a few moments does it glow in rose color, then it burns white and radiates heat to burn the mists from the river, the dampness from the air and the dew from the grasses.

Hippos burp their tuba laugh, the swallows pirouette in the windows of sunlight just beginning to pierce the westerly surfaces of the brown Mara riverbanks.

Impala, gazelle and antelope have been taking this moisture off the grasses since first light; now they pause to rest, to ruminate. And so the sun stirs the lions to seek deep shade for the remainder of the hot day to come.

Overleaf: A low bank of clouds reflects a dusty, glorious Kodachrome sunrise framed by acacia trees.   143

JOURNAL ENTRY

Rhinoceroses are limited to clear vision of twenty-five feet, so the three rhinos sixty yards upwind could only strain their ears while attempting to catch our swirling scent as they peered our way into the sun.

It's the rarity and prehistoric leaning of this species that fascinates me. Their lives are not particularly photogenic, and often their photographs tend to look like a dark lump in a bright landscape.

Although when they decide to move, they can disappear or appear in your face quite quickly (the former is preferred).

We watched these rhinos—a male, female and her quite formidable offspring—as they napped, looked at us or browsed on young acacia trees until they finally decided to disappear through the vegetation into the night shadows.

At dusk, thunderheads billowed in the eastern sky. Gray rain obscured the horizon, while tall masses of swelling cotton-appearing clouds walled up in dangerous formations too violent for a plane to fly into.

As the sun set, pinks retreated up onto higher and higher clouds until there were only various shades of grays remaining.

JOURNAL ENTRY

I hit the 200-roll mark this morning. It's been a very good trip.

Rhinos usually have just one calf—every two to four years.

Overleaf: Poor eyesight is balanced by the white rhinoceros' superb hearing and smell. Once grown, a rhino has no natural predators.

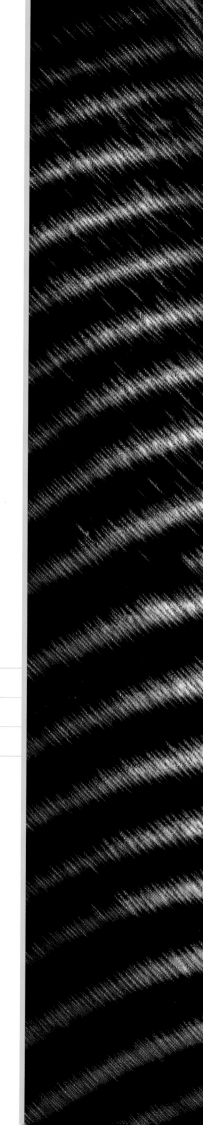

JOURNAL ENTRY

This is one of my last bursts of photographic energy, with a deserving species—the black rhino.

And we were lucky enough to spend several days observing a particular female named Maringo at the Ngare Sergoi Rhino Sanctuary.

Maringo is eleven years old and weighs about three tons. She travels alone and sometimes scares herself when strange noises can't be identified on the wind by her keen nose. Her eyesight is pitiful, only clear to twenty-five feet. It's a wonder this mammal has survived naturally to now.

She possesses a prehensile lip, which she uses to tear branches from her favorite acacia tree; then she takes these whole branches into her mouth like a spaghetti noodle would be chewed. The amazing thing to watch is the stout three- to five-inch thorns going into her mouth as she eats the branch, leaves and thorns without difficulty.

Our lady ate her fill, wandered off to a river gully to water and sleep in the cooler shade.

She's not always this tranquil, however.

On another occasion she has flinched quick as an antelope, moving her body into an alert position and repositioning herself three feet distant in that same instant.

The winds were swirling, so she tromped, fast and powerful as a train locomotive, churning up dust and debris as she ran headlong in a zigzag fashion.

Heaven help the animal that doesn't get out of her way, pronto. I have never watched as solid an animal move so rapidly and so powerfully as this rhino. Even the elephants and buffalos must concern themselves with a rhino on the rampage—one-on-one, she is a mighty force.

The square lip is an obvious identification feature of the white rhinoceros. Mud baths protect their skin from sunburn and pesky insects.

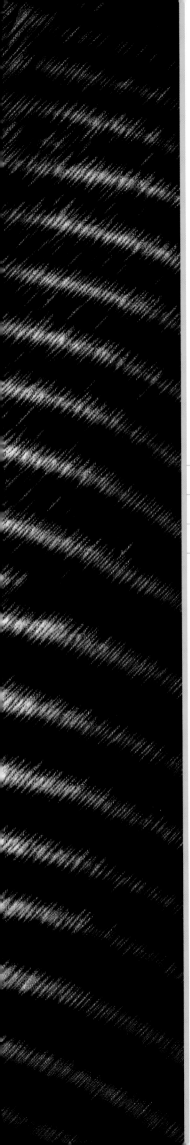

Head down, babies in tow, a mother rhino moved slowly at first, giving us a little saving grace in which to clear away from her and her young, but our Land Rover didn't move an inch.

Now her walking turned into a charge. These kinds of moments become slow-motion replays in my mind. I watched in curiosity when I first saw her moving from behind the brush; she looked so huge compared to her young, compared to anything else in the landscape.

In several milliseconds,
it became clear she was coming
too fast for curiosity.

And the speed at which her young followed suit would scare the daylights out of any creature.

Then, I saw the tail held aloft, the ears so focused and the head being lowered in a powerful momentum. I also saw dust from pounding footsteps as she turned fully sideways at the last moment, moving her speeding train of followers off and away into cover too dense to follow.

All this had taken place in the blink, or unblinking, of an eye. Had my eye been behind the camera, perhaps I would have something quite wonderful to show. Instead, the moment passed so incredulously fast, and I'm left with this slow-motion replay in my brain.

". . . she looked so huge compared to her young,
compared to anything else in the landscape."

JOURNAL ENTRY

What a wonderful morning we had. We saw elephants at a distance making a line through the acacia trees. As they neared, we could see there were five—the matriarch, her baby and three other relatives.

We then saw two other groups off in the distance; they all joined and greeted one another, trunks searching for smells, while completely surrounding our Land Rover.

All the gurgling stomachs, the tearing of branches, the babies bluff-charging the vehicle.

Just to be able to see elephants that close, the wrinkles in their skin, the bottoms of their feet, the hairs on their tail, their long eyelashes—not many people have an experience like this.

Inside the vehicle I feel secure. Because as long as I stay there it acts as a hide, or blind, and the wildlife carries on as if I weren't there. Step outside, and dozens of eyes focus on me. My world enters their world, we merge. Suddenly, I'm aware of my vulnerability. It serves me as a sobering realization, and I will be careful.

The elephants were eating the acacia trees. Literally, coming up to the trees and ripping off whole branches, taking the branch and putting it into the mouth, like a noodle.

Sometimes, we go through forests where the elephants have passed. You can see many of the trees are broken off, with cropped tops, branches mangled. Myriad trees are dead and dying; others are sprouting new branches.

The Serengeti is where the wildlife blends into the grasslands, and the acacia trees stand out in stark contrast.

Baby elephants are full of play. They must learn balance and gain the ability to use their trunks for feeding.

Overleaf: Wildebeest herds can number in the thousands.

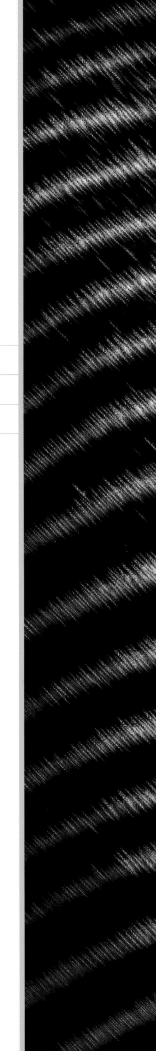

*"Sometimes when you're taking ordinary pictures,
extraordinary things happen."*

Rains come, the game is plentiful, there's lots of hope for life. Often later on, in the dry season, one can see starving little lion kittens. The flip side of all the life here is all of the death here. Sometimes when you're taking ordinary pictures, extraordinary things happen. You just have to be here.

In the vastness of the Serengeti,
it seems one can see forever
or at least until infinity turns to
a violet-gray on the ancient hills
so many miles away.

Rounded and smooth, flowing from one hill to another, weathered by eons of our time, these hills have been worn by endless cycles of dry and wet seasons, by winds and by the pressing of so many generations of footsteps from lions and wildebeest and Masai; now it's the safari Land Rovers, too.

But the land is patient, time eternal; the present cycle will become one with the past and will merge with the future, whatever it may be.

DATE DUE

MAY 2 7 2003			
AUG 2 5 2003			
JUL 1 8 2005			
GAYLORD			PRINTED IN U.S.A.